The Splendor of the Psalms

*Ed,
Love,
Fran*

Answer me when I pray, O God, my defender!
When I was in trouble, you helped me.
Be kind to me now and hear my prayer.

4:1 TEV

The Splendor of the Psalms

A Photographic Meditation

by Herb & Mary Montgomery

I lift up my eyes to the hills.
From whence does my help come?
My help comes from the Lord,
who made heaven and earth.

121:1-2 RSV

Winston Press

ACKNOWLEDGMENTS AND PERMISSIONS

Verses marked TEV are taken from the **Good News Bible** — Old Testament: Copyright © American Bible Society 1976.

Verses marked RSV are taken from the **Revised Standard Version** of the Bible, copyrighted 1946, 1952, © 1971, 1973.

Verses marked KJV are taken from the **King James Version.**

Verses marked TLB are taken from **The Living Bible,** copyright 1971 by Tyndale House Publishers, Wheaton, Illinois. Used by permission.

Verses marked JB are taken from **The Jerusalem Bible,** copyright © 1966 by Darton, Longman & Todd, Ltd. and Doubleday & Company, Inc. Used by permission of the publisher.

Copyright © 1977 by Herb & Mary Montgomery
Library of Congress Catalog Number: 77-78261

ISBN: 0-03-022956-1

All photographs are by Lucille H. Sukalo except the following:
Gene Ahrens: Psalms 146, 96
Herb Montgomery: Cover, Psalms 121, 102, 63, 139, 144, 136, 71 left
Michael Paul: Psalm 138
Cyril A. Reilly: Psalm 94
Vernon Sigl: Psalms 29, 118
John Sukalo: Psalm 51
Wayne Tilley: Psalm 23

Winston Press, 430 Oak Grove, Minneapolis, Minnesota 55403

5   4   3

To those who seek the Lord

THE BEGINNING

Her name and face have slipped into the shadows of my memory, but I still remember her gentle tone as she introduced our class to the Psalms. "The Lord is my shepherd," she said and then paused while we repeated the words after her in our young voices. "I shall not want," she continued. That was all she asked us to memorize that day before she told us how a shepherd cares for his sheep. Growing up in a rural community I had many experiences of people caring for animals, and the image of a Good Shepherd made a great deal of sense to me.

That simple but inspiring line has stayed with me these many years, and I have had reason to recall it during times of loneliness and pain. Hospitalized once in a foreign country with no relative to visit or console me, I found comfort in this and other lines from the Psalms.

For me, the splendor of the Psalms lies in their ability to encourage people throughout a lifetime and to carry through the centuries a portrait of a God who is personal and approachable. A God who is always with us to give us renewal and hope. Indeed, "The Lord is my shepherd; I shall not want."

The writers of the Psalms were people of great faith. Often written amid war, poverty, oppression, and disease, their poetry literally comes singing to us through the ages. Although many of the Psalms include references to the most woeful of experiences, no lament is ever far removed from words of praise and thanksgiving.

The God of the psalmists is one of "lovingkindness." It is this God who touches and transforms lives, both in the long ago and in the present. This is a God who is personally concerned about us, a God who is dynamic, active, involved in our lives.

In selecting the thoughts we wanted to include in *The Splendor of the Psalms,* we hoped especially to reveal God as a source of personal strength. Like the psalmists of old, we are still a praising, thanking, and requesting people. We are also a lamenting people. We know frustration, sadness, pain, discouragement. Mary and I have attempted to bring together, in words and pictures, psalm-thoughts to help us deal with whatever our life experiences may include. Here are thoughts to pray and live by.

The Psalms, it seems to me, speak—better than almost any other writings—to our search for stability in a changing world. They reveal what it means to believe in a loving God who never deceives or abandons us. It is our hope that *The Splendor of the Psalms* will encourage and inspire you, for God is present to touch and transform us whenever we are ready.

Herb Montgomery

Be still, and know that I am God.

46:10 RSV

To you alone, O Lord, to you alone,
    and not to us, must glory be given
    because of your constant love and faithfulness.

115:1 TEV

Lord, you have been
our refuge age after age.
Before the mountains were born,
before the earth or the world came to birth,
you were God from all eternity and for ever.

90:1-2 JB

Of old thou didst lay the foundation of the earth,
    and the heavens are the work of thy hands.
They will perish, but thou dost endure;
    they will all wear out like a garment.
Thou changest them like raiment, and they pass away;
    but thou art the same, and thy years have no end.

102:25-27 RSV

When I look at thy heavens, the work of thy fingers,
     the moon and the stars which thou hast established;
what is man that thou art mindful of him,
     and the son of man that thou dost care for him?

Yet thou hast made him little less than God,
     and dost crown him with glory and honor.
Thou hast given him dominion over the works of thy hands;
     thou hast put all things under his feet,
all sheep and oxen,
     and also the beasts of the field,
the birds of the air, and the fish of the sea,
     whatever passes along the paths of the sea.

O Lord, our Lord,
     how majestic is thy name in all the earth!

8:3-9 RSV

I recall the days of old,
I reflect on all that you did,
I ponder your deeds;
I stretch out my hands,
like thirsty ground I yearn for you.

143:5-6 JB

O God, my God! How I search for you!
How I thirst for you in this parched and weary land
where there is no water. How I long to find you!
How I wish I could go into your sanctuary
to see your strength and glory,
for your love and kindness are better
to me than life itself. How I praise you!
I will bless you as long as I live,
lifting up my hands to you in prayer.
At last I shall be fully satisfied;
I will praise you with great joy.

63:1-5 TLB

I need only say, "I am slipping,"
and your love, Lord, immediately supports me;
and in the middle of all my troubles
you console me and make me happy.

94:18-19 JB

God not only heard me,
he listened to my prayer.

Blessed be God,
who neither ignored my prayer
nor deprived me of his love.

66:19-20 JB

Praise the Lord!
Praise the Lord from the heavens,
    praise him in the heights!
Praise him, all his angels,
    praise him, all his host!

. . .

Praise the Lord from the earth,
    you sea monsters and all deeps,
fire and hail, snow and frost,
    stormy wind fulfilling his command!

Mountains and all hills,
    fruit trees and all cedars!
Beasts and all cattle,
    creeping things and flying birds!

Kings of the earth and all peoples,
    princes and all rulers of the earth!
Young men and maidens together,
    old men and children!

Let them praise the name of the Lord,
    for his name alone is exalted;
    his glory is above earth and heaven.

. . .

Praise the Lord!

148 RSV

It was you who created my inmost self,
and put me together in my mother's womb;
for all these mysteries I thank you:
for the wonder of myself,
for the wonder of your works.

139:13-14 JB

God's laws are perfect. They protect us, make us wise, and give us joy and light. God's laws are pure, eternal, just. They are more desirable than gold. They are sweeter than honey dripping from a honeycomb. For they warn us away from harm and give success to those who obey them.

But how can I ever know what sins are lurking in my heart? Cleanse me from these hidden faults. And keep me from deliberate wrongs; help me to stop doing them. Only then can I be free of guilt and innocent of some great crime.

May my spoken words and unspoken thoughts be pleasing even to you, O Lord my Rock and my Redeemer.

19:7-14 TLB

Create in me a clean heart, O God;
and renew a right spirit within me.
Cast me not away from thy presence;
and take not thy holy spirit from me.

51:10-11 KJV

I am listening. What is the Lord saying?

85:8 JB

Lord, I have given up my pride
    and turned away from my arrogance.
I am not concerned with great matters
    or with subjects too difficult for me.
Instead, I am content and at peace.
As a child lies quietly in its mother's arms,
    so my heart is quiet within me.

131:1-2 TEV

He is like a father to us,
tender and sympathetic to those who reverence him.
For he knows we are but dust,
and that our days are few and brief, like grass,
like flowers, blown by the wind and gone forever.

But the lovingkindness of the Lord
is from everlasting to everlasting,
to those who reverence him.

103:13-17 TLB

The dead cannot sing praises to God
here on earth, but we can!
We praise him forever!
Hallelujah! Praise the Lord!

115:17-18 TLB

I know that I will live to see
    the Lord's goodness in this present life.
Trust in the Lord.
    Have faith, do not despair.
Trust in the Lord.

27:13-14 TEV

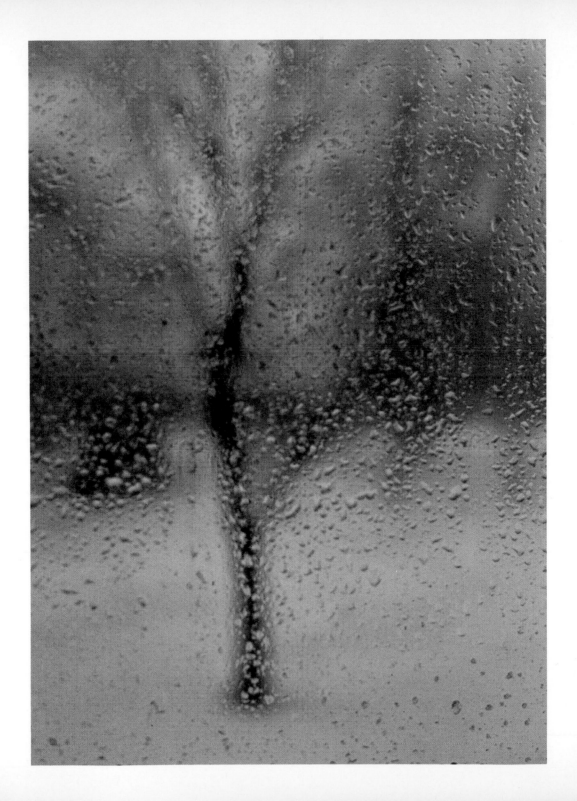

May our sons in their youth
    be like plants that grow up strong.
May our daughters be like stately columns
    which adorn the corners of a palace.
May our barns be filled with crops of every kind.
May the sheep in our fields
    bear young by the tens of thousands.
May our cattle reproduce plentifully
    without miscarriage or loss.
May there be no cries of distress in our streets.

Happy is the nation of whom this is true;
    happy are the people whose God is the Lord!

144:12-15 TEV

The Lord will give strength unto his people;
the Lord will bless his people with peace.

29:11 KJV

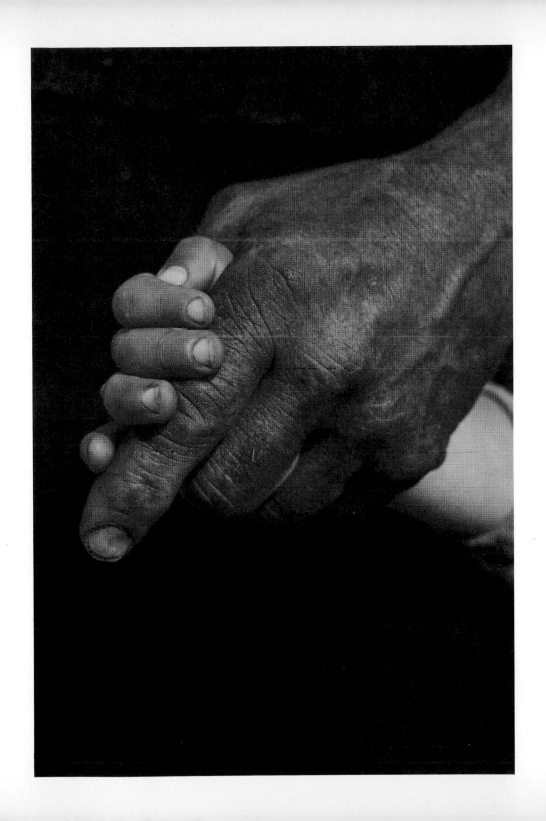

God, forever faithful,
gives justice to those denied it,
gives food to the hungry,
gives liberty to prisoners.

God restores sight to the blind,
God straightens the bent,
God protects the stranger,
he keeps the orphan and widow.

God loves the virtuous,
and frustrates the wicked.
God reigns for ever.

146:6-10 JB

Blessed is every one who fears the Lord,
    who walks in his ways!
You shall eat the fruit of the labor of your hands;
    you shall be happy, and it shall be well with you.

128:1-2 RSV

Trust in the Lord and do good;
     live in the land and be safe.
Seek your happiness in the Lord,
     and he will give you your heart's desire.

37:3-4 TEV

Turn away from evil and do good,
     and your descendants will always live in the land;
for the Lord loves what is right
     and does not abandon his faithful people.
He protects them forever.

37:27-28 TEV

I was filled with fear and anxiety.
Then I called to the Lord,
　　"I beg you, Lord, save me!"

The Lord is merciful and good;
　　our God is compassionate.
The Lord protects the helpless;
　　when I was in danger, he saved me.
Be confident, my heart,
　　because the Lord has been good to me.
　　　　　. . .
And so I walk in the presence of the Lord
　　in the world of the living.

116:3-9 TEV

O God, my heart is ready to praise you! I will sing and rejoice before you.

Wake up, O harp and lyre! We will meet the dawn with song. I will praise you everywhere around the world, in every nation. For your lovingkindness is great beyond measure, high as the heavens.
Your faithfulness reaches the skies.
His glory is far more vast than the heavens.
It towers above the earth.
Hear the cry of your beloved child.

108:1-6 TLB

O give thanks to the Lord,
    for he is good.

        . . .

It is he who remembered us in our low estate,
    for his steadfast love endures forever;
and rescued us from our foes,
    for his steadfast love endures forever;
he who gives food to all flesh,
    for his steadfast love endures forever.

O give thanks to the God of heaven,
    for his steadfast love endures forever.

136:1,23-26 RSV

The Lord is my shepherd; I shall not want.
He maketh me to lie down in green pastures:
he leadeth me beside the still waters.
He restoreth my soul: he leadeth me in the
paths of righteousness for his name's sake.
Yea, though I walk through the valley of the
shadow of death, I will fear no evil:
for thou art with me; thy rod and thy staff
they comfort me.
Thou preparest a table before me in the
presence of mine enemies: thou anointest
my head with oil; my cup runneth over.
Surely goodness and mercy shall follow me
all the days of my life: and I will dwell
in the house of the Lord for ever.

23 KJV

Lord, I have trusted you
since my youth,
I have relied on you
since I was born.

. . .

Do not reject me
now I am old,
nor desert me
now my strength is failing.

71:5-6,9 JB

Reduced to weakness and poverty,
my heart is sorely tormented;
I am dwindling away like a shadow,
they have brushed me off like a locust.

My knees are weak...,
my body is thin...;
I have become an object of derision,
people shake their heads at me in scorn.

Help me, Lord,
save me since you love me,
and let them know that you have done it,
that it was you, Lord, who did it.

109:22-27 JB

I thank you, Lord, with all my heart,
because you have heard what I said.

. . .

The day I called for help, you heard me
and you increased my strength.

138:1,3 JB

Let the heavens be glad, and let the earth rejoice;
　　let the sea roar, and all that fills it;
　　let the field exult, and everything in it!
Then shall all the trees of the wood sing for joy
　　before the Lord, for he comes,
　　for he comes to judge the earth.
He will judge the world with righteousness,
　　and the peoples with his truth.

96:11-13 RSV

This is the day which the Lord hath made;
we will rejoice and be glad in it.

118:24 KJV

From the rising of the sun
unto the going down of the same
the Lord's name is to be praised.

113:3 KJV

Then tell the next generation
that God is here,
our God and leader,
for ever and ever.

48:13-14 JB